Usborne Spo

BIRDS OF PREY

Edited by Michelle Bates and Rick Morris
Series editor: Philippa Wingate
Designed by Helen Wood and Rebecca Mills
Cover designer: Michael Hill
Series designer: Laura Fearn
Illustrations by Alan Harris and Trevor Boyer
Maps by Helen Wood
Peter Holden is National Organizer of the RSPB junior membership
Richard Porter is co-author of "Flight Identification of European Raptors".

The publisher and authors acknowledge their indebtedness
to the following books and journals which were consulted
for reference or as sources of illustrations:
"The Birds of Britain and Europe". H. Heinzel, R.S.R.Fitter & J.L.F.Parslow
(Collins); "The Birds of the Western Palearctic, Vol.II". Edited by S.Cramp &
K.E.L. Simmons (Oxford); "British Birds", Vol 73, pages 239-256. Edited by
J.T.R.Sharrock; "Flight Identification of European Raptors". R.F. Porter, Ian
Willis; Steen Christensen and Bent Pors Nielsen (T. & A.D.Poyser); "Owls of
the World". Edited by J.A.Burton (Peter Lowe).

Acknowledgements: Cover © Kim Taylor/Warren Photographic;
1 © Corbis /Hannu Hautala; Frank Lane Picture Agency; 2-3 © Corbis /W
Perry Conway; 8-9 © Corbis /Eric and David Hosking; 10-11 © Digital Vision;
58-59 © Digital Vision; 60-61 © Corbis /Joe Macdonald; thanks to Digital
Vision for the background pictures on pages 4-7, 12-57, 60-64.

CONTENTS

HOW TO USE THIS BOOK

This book is an identification guide to the birds of prey in the British Isles and Europe. Each bird in this book has a picture and a description to help you to identify it. The description gives you information about any special markings, where the bird can be found and what it feeds on, along with its average wingspan. There is a circle beside each picture to tick when you have spotted that species of bird of prey. Here is a sample description.

➡ SPARROWHAWK
Wingspan 60cm.
The male is blue-grey above and barred reddish below. The female is larger, and brown above with darker brown barring below. Juvenile has streaked underparts. Hunts small birds in flight.

——Circle for ticking

♂

♀

The map shows where you will find the bird (see opposite)

This shows the female Sparrowhawk, which has different markings from the male

This picture gives more information about the bird's habits

Throughout this book, you will find suggested links to birds of prey websites. For a complete list of links and instructions, turn to page 62.

VARIATIONS

If male and female birds vary, both are shown. The symbol ♀ means female and ♂ means male. Sometimes the young, or "juvenile" bird is shown too, and the "immature" bird (fully grown, but without adult plumage yet).

GLOSSARY

Pages 55-57 show the wing and tail shapes of raptors when seen in flight. On page 60 there is a glossary. Use it to look up any words that you don't know. On page 61 there's a diagram which labels the main parts of a bird that are discussed in the descriptions.

MAPS

The areas shaded in orange show where birds are resident (seen all year round). The areas in yellow and blue show where birds are migrant (present in summer or winter, but visit other parts of Europe too). A partial migrant is when

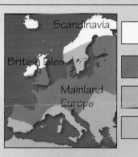

	Present in summer
	Resident all year
	Present in winter
	Not present

some members of a species are migrant while others are resident.

MEASURING BIRDS

There are two main groups of birds of prey: raptors and owls. Raptors are recorded by wingspan (measured from wing-tip to wing-tip), and owls by length (from the tip of the beak to the tip of the tail).

Wingspan 120cm

Raptor

Length 38cm

Owl

5

BIRDS OF PREY

Although many birds eat other animals, the term "birds of prey" usually refers to birds that have hooked bills and curved claws (called talons) designed for killing. The pictures on these pages show the main differences between the two main groups of birds of prey.

RAPTORS

Raptors hunt by day. Some of their main distinguishing features are shown on the Rough-legged Buzzard and the Hobby below.

Rough-legged Buzzard

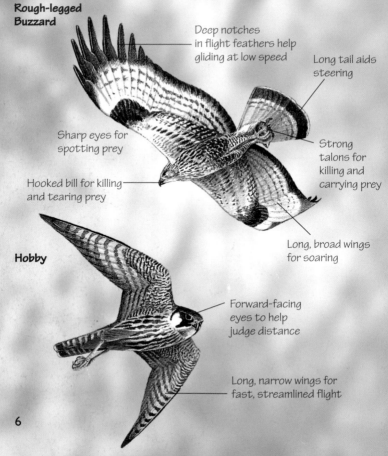

Deep notches in flight feathers help gliding at low speed

Long tail aids steering

Sharp eyes for spotting prey

Strong talons for killing and carrying prey

Hooked bill for killing and tearing prey

Long, broad wings for soaring

Hobby

Forward-facing eyes to help judge distance

Long, narrow wings for fast, streamlined flight

For a link to audio and video clips of birds of prey, turn to page 62.

OWLS

Most species of owls hunt after sunset. Some of their distinguishing features are shown on the Long-eared Owl and Barn Owl below.

Long-eared Owl

Facial disc funnels sound to aid hearing

Tufts of feathers for display

Hooked bill for tearing prey

Large eyes to see prey at night. They are forward-facing eyes to help judge distance

Head can turn right round and back again

Camouflage to hide the bird during the day

Talons for killing. Outer toe can face forwards, or backwards to help grip prey

Barn Owl

Soft feathers for silent flight

Large ears are used to find prey. They are normally hidden by feathers

7

HUNTING

All birds of prey are well-equipped as hunters. Their vision can be up to eight times as sharp as human vision, enabling them to spot their prey from a distance. They also have strong, sharp talons to help them catch and kill their prey, and hooked beaks to help them tear its flesh.

Birds of prey hunt differently, according to the type of prey they are aiming for. They have different characteristics to help them catch that particular prey.
For example:

• The Eagle Owl has large, very strong toes and talons for catching, gripping and killing large prey up to the size of a fox.

• The Hobby chases and catches prey in the air.

• The Honey Buzzard's feet are used for digging out wasps' and bees' nests so they do not need to have curved talons or a strong grip.

• Vultures soar on outstretched wings using up-currents of air. They scan large areas of country for prey.

• The Tawny Owl watches and listens from a perch and then swoops onto prey.

- The Sparrowhawk has long, slender legs with wide, spreading feet to give it a longer reach for catching small, agile birds in flight. It surprises prey with a quick dash from cover.

- The Osprey's feet must catch and grip slippery, wriggling fish. Long, curved talons and sharp spines beneath the toes help it to do so. The Osprey dives, feet first, for fish swimming just below the surface of the water.

- The Kestrel hovers, moving wings and tail, but keeping the head and eyes quite still to spot small movements on the ground below.

- The Peregrine "stoops" (swoops down) at great speed from a height to kill flying birds.

- The Marsh Harrier and the Barn Owl fly low over the ground with slow wing-beats and glides, searching to and fro for prey.

Barn Owl in flight

9

For a link to an interactive food chain game, turn to page 62.

MIGRATION

Migration is the making of regular journeys from one place to another and back again. Some birds of prey migrate in spring and autumn (as do other birds). In Europe birds of prey usually travel between a summer breeding area and a wintering area in Africa.

WHY MIGRATE?

Birds migrate in autumn when food, such as insects, becomes hard to find. It is food shortages rather than cold weather which cause migration.

RETURNING HOME

The birds return in spring when food supplies have built up again. By doing so, the birds feed better and face less competition for food from other animals. If they travel northwards, they have more daylight in which to hunt and feed their young.

IRRUPTIONS

Irruptions are irregular journeys from the usual range. They are usually caused by changes in the food supply. Snowy Owls, for instance, irrupt well to the south of their normal wintering range when their usual food sources are scarce.

RECORDING BIRDS

Much of our information about migration comes from ringing schemes in which birds are caught and carefully fitted with metal leg rings by trained ringers. Each ring bears a unique number and address. Finding and reporting ringed birds tells us a great deal about the age and movement of the birds. Wing tags bearing numbers or letters can be read with binoculars so that the birds don't need to be caught. Tracking individual birds on their flight paths is also possible if a small radio transmitter is attached to each bird.

Lammergeier in flight

RAPTORS

➡ HONEY BUZZARD

Wingspan 140cm. Medium-sized raptor. Differs from Buzzard in shape by having a longer neck and longer tail. Plumage colour varies. Visits old woodlands in summer. Rare in Britain.

Adults are barred below with black bands on their flight feathers and tail

Soars with wings held flat, not in a shallow "V" like a Buzzard

Diet includes wasp and other insect larvae. Stiff feathers protect face from stings

In autumn the birds migrate in large flocks to Africa

Migrant

12

➡ BLACK-SHOULDERED KITE

Wingspan 80cm. Kestrel-sized raptor. Grey and white with black shoulders and black tips on the under-wing. Found in open countryside with scattered trees. Rare in most of Europe.

When not hunting, often perches in trees or on telegraph poles

Juvenile

Feeds on small mammals, birds and large insects

Adult dropping onto prey

Immature

Resident

Often hovers when hunting and then drops onto prey. Flies with fast wing-beats, then glides on slightly raised wings

13

RAPTORS

➡ BLACK KITE

Wingspan 170cm. Larger than Buzzard. Dark brown all over. Unlike the Red Kite, it isn't red-brown with white wing patches. Found in varying habitats, from woods to towns, often near water. Feeds on carrion.

Longer, narrower wings and longer tail than Buzzard. Note shallow, forked tail

Soars with wings held flat, not in shallow "V" like a Buzzard

Nests in trees or on buildings

Migrant

In autumn, the birds migrate in large flocks to Africa

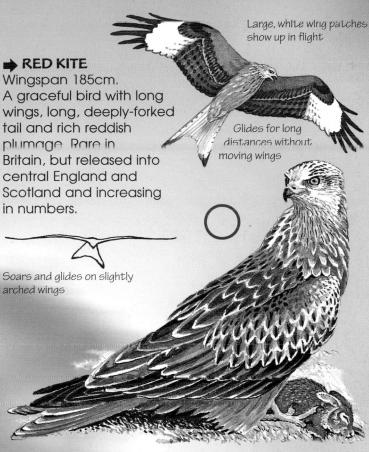

Large, white wing patches show up in flight

➡ RED KITE
Wingspan 185cm.
A graceful bird with long wings, long, deeply-forked tail and rich reddish plumage. Rare in Britain, but released into central England and Scotland and increasing in numbers.

Glides for long distances without moving wings

Soars and glides on slightly arched wings

Feeds largely on dead animals, but also kills live creatures including earthworms

Mostly migratory, but resident in Britain

Red Kites breed in old woodlands

RAPTORS

➡ WHITE-TAILED EAGLE

Wingspan 220cm. A large, powerful, brown eagle with broad, "doormat-like" wings, massive bill and short, white tail. Likes rocky sea coasts, but also rivers and lakes in eastern Europe.

Adult

Immature

Persecuted in parts of Europe until it became extinct in Britain but has now been reintroduced into Scotland

Immature is patchy below and has a dark tail

Largely resident

An adult taking a waterbird. They also feed on fish, mammals and carrion

"Beard" visible only at close range

➡ LAMMERGEIER or BEARDED VULTURE

The wingspan of 275cm is the largest of any European vulture. Has long, rather pointed wings and diamond-shaped tail. Lives in remote mountains and steep gorges.

"Beard"

Adults often have orange-yellow heads and underparts, but some adults have paler heads

Adult

Juveniles are darker than adults

The Lammergeier feeds on the flesh of dead animals. It drops bones to crack them to reach the marrow inside

Largely resident

17

RAPTORS

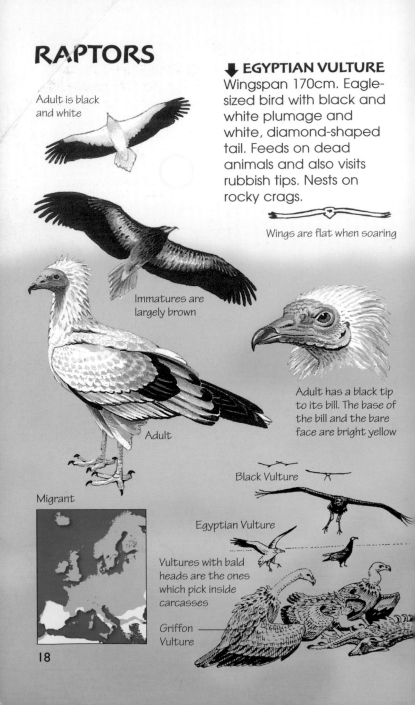

Adult is black and white

⬇ EGYPTIAN VULTURE

Wingspan 170cm. Eagle-sized bird with black and white plumage and white, diamond-shaped tail. Feeds on dead animals and also visits rubbish tips. Nests on rocky crags.

Wings are flat when soaring

Immatures are largely brown

Adult has a black tip to its bill. The base of the bill and the bare face are bright yellow

Adult

Migrant

Black Vulture

Egyptian Vulture

Vultures with bald heads are the ones which pick inside carcasses

Griffon Vulture

Wings held in shallow "V" when soaring

Ginger-brown wing coverts contrast with dark flight feathers

Mainly resident

⬇ GRIFFON VULTURE

Wingspan 250cm. Much larger than the Egyptian Vulture. Often gathers in soaring parties while searching for carrion. Nests in colonies on cliff ledges. Juveniles look similar to adults.

Bare head and neck for reaching inside carcasses

Wings held flat when soaring

Huge, black, with short neck and tail

⬇ BLACK VULTURE

Wingspan 270cm. Larger than the Griffon Vulture. Occurs singly or in pairs. Like other vultures, it is becoming rare in Europe because better farming methods leave fewer dead animals.

Resident

Black Vulture

Immature Black Vulture

Head of adult looks pale only at close range

19

For a link to the Peregrine Fund's raptor photos and facts, turn to page 62.

RAPTORS

➡ SHORT-TOED EAGLE

Wingspan 190cm. Large, pale eagle which often hovers when hunting. Migrates singly or in small parties. Leaves Europe in September and winters in Africa.

Very pale underparts with some dark marks

Some birds have dark heads

Feeds on reptiles, especially snakes. Needs to catch one or two snakes each day

Migrant

Lives in dry, open country with scattered trees

Males are grey, brown and chestnut

➡ **MARSH HARRIER**

Wingspan 125cm. Buzzard-sized bird, but has slimmer wings and longer tail. Lives in reed beds and marshes. Flies with several wing-beats, followed by a glide with wings held in a shallow "V".

Typical flight path

Females and juveniles are dark brown, often with yellow on heads and wings

Feeds on birds, voles, frogs and other marshland animals

Largely migratory

During spectacular display-flights harriers will sometimes grip talons with each other

21

RAPTORS

➡ HEN HARRIER
Wingspan 110cm. Breeds in open country, often on upland moors. Like other harriers, its flight seems lazy, with a few wing-beats followed by a glide with wings held in a shallow "V".

Female has owl-like face, surrounded by a "ruff" of feathers

♀

♀

Male has dark, trailing edge to wings

♂

Male is silver-grey with black wing-tips

♂

Heavier and broader wings than Pallid and Montagu's Harriers

Partial migrant

♀

Hen Harriers fly low, looking and listening for voles and other prey

➡ PALLID HARRIER

Wingspan 100cm. Breeds on grasslands and plains in eastern Europe. A lightly built, slim-winged, long-tailed raptor. Feeds on small mammals and birds, insects and reptiles.

Migrant

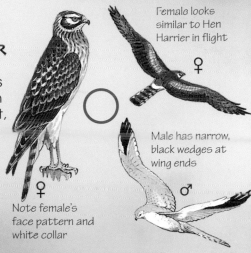

Female looks similar to Hen Harrier in flight

♀

Male has narrow, black wedges at wing ends

♂

Note female's face pattern and white collar

♀

⬇ MONTAGU'S HARRIER

Wingspan 110cm. Occasionally visits Britain in summer. Becoming rare throughout Europe. Breeds on grassland and in cereal fields. Feeds on mammals and birds. Male is dirtier grey than Pallid Harrier.

Male has black wing-ends, black wing-bar and rusty streaks on flanks

♂

Female is similar to Pallid Harrier in flight

♀

Migrant

Female has pale face patch and no white collar

♀

Hunts close to the ground

RAPTORS

➡ **GOSHAWK**

Wingspan 150cm.
Looks like a large,
powerful Sparrowhawk.
Lives in woodland, hunts
in open areas. Young
birds are streaked
below. Goshawks
have a broad, white
stripe over the eye.

White patch
under tail
shows in flight

Feeds mainly on
medium-sized
birds, such as
pigeons and crows

Jay

♀

Female is much larger
than the male

Largely resident

A Goshawk seizes
a Woodpigeon
after a short,
fast chase

➡ SPARROWHAWK

Wingspan 60cm. Male is blue-grey above, barred reddish below. Larger female is brown above with darker brown barring below. Juvenile has streaked underparts. Hunts small birds in flight.

Partial migrant

Sparrowhawk woodland birds that also visit towns and gardens

♂

♀

Wings are short and rounded; tail is long

Flies with rapid wing-beats and short glides

⬇ LEVANT SPARROWHAWK

Wingspan 70cm. Female is similar to a Sparrowhawk, but wing-tips are darker and more pointed. Back of male is blue-grey, underparts are white, tinged with pink. Hunts lizards and large insects.

Summer migrant

Male has black wing-tips

♂

♂

♀

Migrates to Africa in large flocks in September

25

For a link to birds of prey audio clips, facts and photos, turn to page 62.

are
t

D

Wingspan 120cm.
Smaller than an eagle,
and one of the most
widespread raptors in
Europe. Most common
in hilly areas with woods.
Also found on farmland.
Varies in colour from
pale to very dark.

Pale form is the commonest in northern Europe

Typical form. Note brown underparts, paler flight feathers and barred tail

Often soars with wings raised in shallow "V"

Feeds on small mammals, birds, insects, worms and also carrion

Partial migrant

Buzzards from eastern and northern Europe migrate to Africa in large flocks in autumn

26

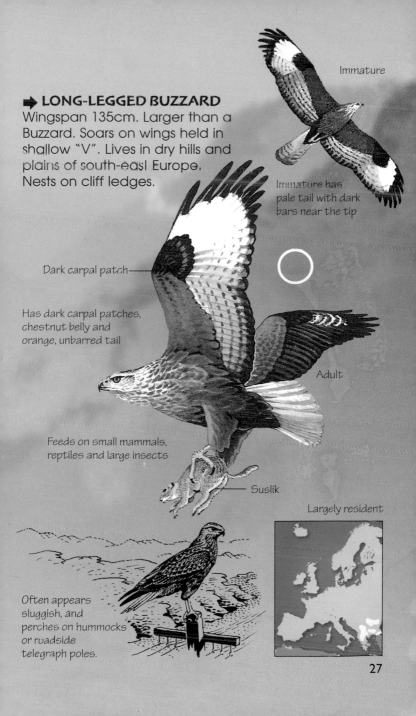

➡ **LONG-LEGGED BUZZARD**

Wingspan 135cm. Larger than a Buzzard. Soars on wings held in shallow "V". Lives in dry hills and plains of south-east Europe. Nests on cliff ledges.

Immature

Immature has pale tail with dark bars near the tip

Dark carpal patch

Has dark carpal patches, chestnut belly and orange, unbarred tail

Adult

Feeds on small mammals, reptiles and large insects

Suslik

Largely resident

Often appears sluggish, and perches on hummocks or roadside telegraph poles.

27

RAPTORS

➡ **ROUGH-LEGGED BUZZARD**

Wingspan 130cm. Lives on the Arctic plains. Larger and usually paler than other buzzards. More birds are seen during certain "invasion years" than at other times. A few birds reach Britain in autumn.

Dark carpal patch

Note dark belly patch, dark carpal patches and white tail with black band

Feeds mainly on mammals caught on the ground

Lemming

Often hovers when searching for prey

Migrant

Pairs "sky-dance" as they display in spring

28

➡ LESSER SPOTTED EAGLE

Wingspan 150cm. An all-brown eagle, which breeds in the old forests of eastern Europe. Migrates in large flocks, arriving in March or April and leaving in September.

Migrant

Flight feathers are darker than under-wing coverts

Adult

Soars on slightly bowed wings

Juvenile

Eats small mammals, birds, frogs and snakes

Young birds have white spots on their wings

⬇ SPOTTED EAGLE

Wingspan 170cm. A darker and bulkier bird than the more common Lesser Spotted Eagle. It breeds in old, damp woodlands. Not seen in flocks when migrating. Visits marshes in winter.

Migrant

Soars with flat wings and drooping primaries

Adult

Under-wing coverts are usually darker than flight feathers

Juveniles have many white spots on wings

Eats wide range of animals including ducks and coots

29

For a link to fun online activities on the RSPB Kids Website, turn to page 62.

RAPTORS

➡ IMPERIAL EAGLE

Wingspan 200cm. Similar in size to a Golden Eagle. Lives in open countryside with scattered trees. Found in a few parts of southern Europe. Adult identified by white "braces". Two different-looking races breed in Europe.

Juvenile is streaked sandy-brown with a pale patch on dark flight feathers

Eastern race juvenile

Lesser Kestrel

Adult being mobbed by male Lesser Kestrel

Spanish race adult

"Braces"

Eastern race adult

"Braces" are less defined on Eastern race. Only adult of Spanish race has white leading edge to wings

Largely resident but immatures may be partial migrants

➡ GOLDEN EAGLE
Wingspan 210cm.
Large, powerful eagle
that lives in remote hills
and mountains. Feeds on
medium-sized mammals
such as hares, birds such
as grouse, and carrion
such as dead lambs.

Juvenile has white
patches on its
wings and tail

Juvenile

Soars effortlessly
on wings raised in a
shallow "V"

Adult is dark
brown with gold
crown and nape

Adult

Mountain Hare

Mainly resident

Usually only
one eaglet
is raised to
the flying
stage from
each nest

31

RAPTORS

➡ BOOTED EAGLE

Wingspan 110cm. Two kinds are found in Europe: a light one and a dark one. Soars and glides on wings held flat. Looks similar to the female Marsh Harrier except that the Marsh Harrier holds wings in shallow "V".

White feathers on legs give this raptor its name

Soars and glides on flat wings

Light birds have pale underparts with black flight feathers

Dark birds are dark brown with pale tail and pale "wedge" on wings

Migrant

Pairs perform spectacular display-flights over woods in spring

Adults have white patch on their backs

➡ BONELLI'S EAGLE

Wingspan 165cm. Powerful, medium-sized eagle. Like Booted Eagle, adult is brown above and whitish below, with dark streaks on underparts. Soars and glides on wings held flat.

Young birds look similar to Buzzard but larger with longer wings and tail, and head protruding further in front of wings

Juvenile

Catches medium-sized birds and mammals

Adults are whitish below, with black band on tail, and usually a broad black band on underside of wings

Resident

Often seen in pairs over rocky mountain areas

33

For a link to live webcam footage of a family of eagles, turn to page 62.

RAPTORS

➡ MERLIN

Wingspan 55cm. Similar in shape to a Kestrel, but with shorter wings. It is Europe's smallest falcon and lives in open country, usually moorland. It moves to coastal marshes in winter. Feeds mainly on small birds.

Male is soft blue-grey above, with a dark band at the end of the tail

♂

♀

Prefers to nest on the ground. Some nesting areas may have been in use for many years

♂

Female is brown above and streaked below with bands on the tail

Male has reddish underparts

Partial migrant

Carry off

Snatch

Chase

The Merlin hunts small birds in a spectacular dashing chase

➡ HOBBY

Wingspan 85cm. A small falcon with long, pointed wings and a short tail. It may often look like a large Swift. Nests in pine trees, using old nests of other birds such as crows.

The Hobby catches prey with its feet and often feeds in flight

Adults are blue-grey above with dark streaks on underparts.

Juvenile

Juvenile is like adult but browner with less colourful "trousers"

Note black "moustache" and red "trousers"

Migrant

A Hobby chasing two Swifts. Hobbies feed mainly on insects and small birds which they catch in flight

35

RAPTORS

➡ RED-FOOTED FALCON
Wingspan 70cm. Similar in size and shape to a Hobby. Frequently hovers. Plumage varies depending on age and sex. Breeds in colonies and uses old nests of other birds such as Rooks.

Juvenile

Adult

♂

Male is slate-grey with red "trousers"

Juvenile is similar to female, but with dark crown, streaked underparts and dark rear edge to wings

Female's head, underparts and under-wing coverts are orange-yellow

♀

Catches insects in flight, often over marshland

Migrant

Parties often hunt insects at dusk

➡ ELEONORA'S FALCON

Wingspan 110cm. Between Hobby and Peregrine in size. Two distinct colours are found in Europe. Breeds in autumn so that young may be fed on small migrant birds returning south.

Wheatear

Nests on rocky cliffs around the Mediterranean

The light-coloured bird is similar to Hobby, but has dark under-wing coverts and lacks red "trousers"

Dark-coloured bird is all dark with even darker wing coverts

Migrant

Feeds on small birds which are caught in flight

37

RAPTORS

➡ LESSER KESTREL

Wingspan 65cm. Nests in
colonies, breeding in holes
in walls and under eaves.
Feeds mainly on flying insects
which it catches in flight.
A shrill *kit-kit-kit* call.

♂

Male has
no moustache,
unspotted back,
and blue on upper wing

Nests are often
built in ruined
buildings

♂

Female Lesser Kestrel
is difficult to tell
from female Kestrel
unless you see her
white claws

♀

Large feeding
parties hunt
at dusk

Migrant

➡ KESTREL

Wingspan 75cm. One of our commonest birds of prey, found in open country and in some towns. May be seen hovering beside busy roads. Catches small mammals and insects on the ground.

Male has black "moustache" and spots on reddish back

♂

♀

Female has barred tail and darker, streaked underparts

♀

Regularly hovers when hunting, head into wind and tail fanned

Resident and partial migrant

Nestboxes replace natural nest sites on Dutch lowlands

39

RAPTORS

➡ LANNER

Wingspan 110cm.
Large falcon which looks
similar to a Saker. Back
and wings are rather
dark brownish-grey.
Likes open countryside.

Bolder "moustache"
than Saker and also
has reddish-brown
on crown and nape.

Pale below
with dark
streaks. Wing
coverts usually
darker spotted
than rest of
under-wing

Adult Lanner
chasing a
Rock Dove

Rock Dove

Lanners feed mainly
on medium-sized
birds caught in flight

Mainly resident

Lives on rocky
slopes or
stony plains

40

➡ SAKER

Wingspan 110cm.
A large falcon, slightly
bigger than a Perogrine,
Lives on open plains. Upper
parts are pale grey-brown,
not unlike those of a
female Kestrel.
Feeds mostly on
small mammals.

Whitish, streaked crown and
a less noticeable "moustache"
than a Lanner

Pale breast and belly with dark
streaks. Under-wing is pale with
dark tip and dark band of
spots on wing coverts

It is very
difficult to distinguish
between a Lanner and
Saker in flight

Partial migrant

When migrating
it often perches
on telegraph
poles or ruins

41

RAPTORS

➡ GYRFALCON

Wingspan 150cm. This fast and powerful bird is the largest falcon in Europe. It lives in northern, rocky plains and rarely comes south. There are three forms: dark, grey and white.

Adult grey form

Grey and dark forms may resemble a Peregrine, but don't have black "moustache"

Adult white form

Teal

Feeds mostly on birds taken in flight such as Teal

Gyrs can easily kill a Teal or even a Ptarmigan

Immature white form

Partial migrant

Ptarmigan

42

For a link to webcam images of Peregrine falcons, turn to page 62.

Juveniles have brown upper parts

Juvenile

➡ PEREGRINE

Wingspan 100cm.
A powerful pigeon-sized falcon. Flight is rapid, but often soars and glides. Its numbers fell in the 1950s and 60s, due to the effects of toxic chemicals, but are now increasing. Nests on cliff and rock faces and will use buildings too.

Hunts birds in flight. Often "stoops", reaching speeds of over 160kph (100mph)

Adult stooping

Look for pointed wings with broad base, and tapering tail

Rock Dove

Striking a Rock Dove

Adult is blue-grey above with paler, barred underparts

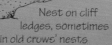

Nest on cliff ledges, sometimes in old crows' nests

Mainly resident

43

RAPTORS

➡ OSPREY

Wingspan 150cm. The only European raptor to feed mainly on fish. Persecuted to extinction in Britain, but now breeding again in Scotland under close protection. It spends winter in Africa.

Eagle-sized, with long, narrow, angled wings

Note brown upperparts, and white underparts with dark wing patches

It catches a fish with a spectacular dive and then carries it "torpedo-fashion" in one or both feet

Undersides of feet are coated with stiff spines to help grip fish

Migrant

Ospreys nest on large stick-built eyries, usually returning each year

OWLS

➜ BARN OWL

Length 34cm. A night hunter, with a monkey-like face. Its call is an eerie screech. Usually lives on farmland and open country, Has a low and wavering flight when hunting. Sometimes hovers over prey.

In Britain, Barn Owls have honey-brown backs and white underparts

Feeds on small mammals and birds

Often nests in barns, old buildings or holes in trees

Continental birds have brown breasts

Resident

Its flight is almost silent

OWLS

➡ EAGLE OWL

Wingspan 70cm. This large, powerful owl lives in dense forests or craggy mountain areas. It will not tolerate other birds of prey nesting in its territory. Its call is a deep *oo-oo-oo*.

Ear-tufts not visible in flight

Hunts mainly mammals and birds. It may kill large prey, up to the size of Roe Deer

Rarely seen in daylight unless disturbed from its roost

Largely resident

Sometimes seen at dusk, silhouetted against the sky, tail cocked and calling

➡ SNOWY OWL
Length 60cm.
Unmistakeable, large
white owl found on the
high, Arctic plains.
Active during daylight.
Often sits on posts or rocks
in the open. Rare visitor to
the British mainland.

♂

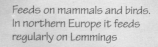

○

♀

Feeds on mammals and birds.
In northern Europe it feeds
regularly on Lemmings

Female is larger and
browner than the male

Partial migrant

Young hatch at intervals. In years when
food is short only the eldest survives

47

OWLS

➡ HAWK OWL

Length 38cm. Found in the conifer forests of northern Europe. Moves into central Europe in winter. Call is a shrill *ki-ki-ki*. Feeds on small mammals and birds.

Often perches in the tops of trees

Note finely barred underparts and a black border to pale facial discs

Short, pointed wings and long tail

Partial migrant

Looks hawk-like in flight. Often hunts in daylight

➡ LITTLE OWL

Length 22cm. A small owl often seen in daylight perched on roadside telegraph poles or branches. Introduced into Britain in the 19th century. Bobs and bows when curious.

Feeds on small mammals, insects and earthworms

Resident

Flight is bounding, usually close to the ground

⬇ PYGMY OWL

Length 16cm. Smallest European owl. Feeds on small mammals and birds, sometimes catching birds in flight. Call is a soft *whee-whee-whee*.

Has short, white eyebrows

Mainly resident

Hunts and flies mainly at night

Often seen cocking its tail. Lives in conifer woods

49

OWLS

➡ TAWNY OWL

Length 38cm. The most common brown owl in Europe. Hunts at night, but may be mobbed by smaller birds in daytime. Hooting song is well known, but also makes loud *kee-wick* call.

Feeds on small mammals, such as voles and mice, and on birds and frogs

Often nests in holes in trees

Note rounded wings and short tail

Tawny Owls are medium-sized owls, and mottled brown or grey

Resident

Some Tawny Owls now live in towns and cities

50

➡ URAL OWL
Length 61cm. Like a large, pale Tawny Owl, but with a longer tail. Hunts at night in large or small woods. All-black eyes are smaller than Tawny Owl's. Call is a barking *wow-wow-wow*.

Resident

Large, pale facial disc

Pale grey owl with broad, rounded wings

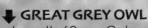

Nests in holes in trees

⬇ GREAT GREY OWL
Length 69cm. Only the Eagle Owl is larger. Lives in dense conifer forests. Call is deep *hu-hu-hoo*. Hunts by day as well as night. Feeds on mammals.

Broad, rounded wings

Uses old nests of birds of prey

Greyish streaked and mottled plumage, large head and small, yellow eyes

Mainly resident

51

OWLS

➡ LONG-EARED OWL
Length 36cm. Rarely seen in daylight. A slim owl with long ear-tufts and orange eyes. Call is long, low, drawn-out *oo-oo-oo*. Call of its young is like the noise of gate swinging on unoiled hinges.

Streaked underparts show in flight, but ear tufts are not visible

Some birds from northern Europe migrate to Britain for the winter

Groups may roost together in winter

Partial migrant

Has zig-zag display-flight. Often nests in thick conifer woods

52

➡ SHORT-EARED OWL

Length 38cm. Ear-tufts are hard to see. Eats voles and other small mammals. In years when voles are numerous, Short-eared Owls produce large families and more birds also winter in the British Isles.

May be seen hunting over moors, marshes and scrub during daylight

Lower breast and belly are whitish

Tired migrants may be seen on dunes after crossing the sea

Slow, wavering flight, with deep wing beats

Often perches on the ground and is less upright than other owls

Partial migrant

Often flies close to the ground and hovers briefly

53

For a link to information, photos and audio clips of owls, turn to page 62.

OWLS

➡️ **TENGMALM'S OWL**
Length 25cm. A night-hunting owl found mainly in conifer woodlands. Feeds on small mammals and birds. Its call is a rapid *poo-poo-poo*.

Young birds are deep brown with bold, white "eyebrows"

Adult

Round head and clearly marked face pattern

Mainly resident

Dark and spotted upperparts, large head and rounded wings

⬇️ **SCOPS OWL**
Length 19cm. Similar in size to the Little Owl, but slimmer and has ear-tufts. Not often seen during the day. At night, its *dwoo, dwoo* call is repeated over and over again.

Its plumage blends with tree trunks and branches

Rarely seen in flight

Migrant

Often heard in southern European towns in summer

RAPTORS IN FLIGHT

Raptors are usually seen In flight, often at a distance. You won't always be able to see the plumage colours but you can tell a lot by the wing and tail shapes and the plumage markings. All, unless otherwise marked, are adults. Four adult eagles look very similar so the different juvenile plumages have been shown. Males ♂ and females ♀ have been shown separately where there is a marked difference between sexes.

VULTURES

Black Vulture

Griffon Vulture

Lammergeier

Egyptian Vulture

EAGLES

White-tailed Eagle

Imperial Eagle – *juvenile*

Golden Eagle – *juvenile*

Short-toed Eagle – *dark-headed*

MORE EAGLES

Bonelli's Eagle

Spotted Eagle – *juvenile*

Lesser Spotted Eagle – *juvenile*

Booted Eagle – *dark form*

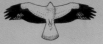

Booted Eagle – *light form*

BUZZARDS

Long-legged Buzzard – *typical adult*

Honey Buzzard – *typical adult*

Rough-legged Buzzard

Buzzard – *typical adult*

KITES

Red Kite

Black-shouldered Kite

Black Kite

HARRIERS

♂

Pallid Harrier

♀

Pallid Harrier

♂

Marsh Harrier

♂

Hen Harrier

♀

Hen Harrier

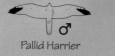

♀   ♂

Montagu's Harrier   Montagu's Harrier

OSPREY

Osprey

HAWKS

Sparrowhawk ♂

Goshawk ♂

Levant Sparrowhawk ♂

Sparrowhawk ♀

Goshawk ♀

FALCONS

Eleonora's falcon – *dark phase*

Gyrfalcon – *white phase*

Eleonora's falcon – *light phase*

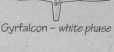
Gyrfalcon – *grey phase*

Saker

Lanner

Peregrine

Kestrel ♂

Merlin ♂

Hobby

Lesser Kestrel ♂

Red-footed Falcon ♀

Red-footed Falcon ♂

57

WHY ARE BIRDS OF PREY RARE?

Many of the places where birds of prey nest and hunt are being destroyed or changed by farming, forestry or building. This has had a damaging effect on their numbers. But even in suitable habitats birds may fail to breed because of disturbance from increasing numbers of people.

Birds of prey are greatly affected by any change in the environment. In the past, a chemical called DDT was widely used to kill insect pests. It killed the insects, but the chemical built up in the bodies of the small birds who ate the insects. For the birds of prey who fed on these small birds, it was fatal. Many of them died or were unable to breed successfully. Today shortages of food can still seriously affect the numbers of birds of prey.

Larger species, such as eagles, often raise just one young each year, and may not begin to breed until they are five years old. Each pair of birds also needs a large area in which to catch their prey.

For a link to information about the threats to birds of prey, turn to page 62.

Sometimes birds of prey are deliberately killed. This is because they are thought (usually quite wrongly) to harm game or domestic animals.

All birds of prey are now legally protected in the UK, and the use of harmful chemicals has been restricted. However, many species are still under threat. Raptors and owls are shot for sport in many parts of Europe and young raptors – especially falcons – are sometimes stolen from the nest for sale or use by falconers.

Organizations such as the RSPB (Royal Society for the Protection of Birds) work hard to protect these species through reintroduction programmes and conserving their habitat.

The Lammergeier is Europe's rarest vulture, but its numbers are now increasing as it is reintroduced into the wild

USEFUL WORDS

This glossary explains some of the more difficult terms used in this book.

carrion – the flesh of a dead animal.

display – courtship behaviour to attract and keep a mate.

eyrie – the nest of a bird of prey. The term is generally used for the large nests of eagles.

immature – a young bird which has grown out of its juvenile plumage but is not yet in adult plumage.

irruptions – irregular journeys from the usual migratory range.

juvenile – a young bird which is in its first full plumage. This plumage is grown while it is still in the nest.

larvae – insects at the stage after hatching from eggs, but before they become full adults.

migrant – a bird that breeds in one area, then moves to another for the winter, returning again the following spring.

partial migrant – when some members of a species are migrant while others are resident.

Black-shouldered Kite on a branch

plumage – all the feathers on a bird.
resident – a bird that can be seen throughout the year.

stoop – a Peregrine's dramatic dive at its prey.
territory – the area defended by a bird, or a pair of birds, for nesting.

PARTS OF A BIRD OF PREY

On the picture below the main parts of a bird's body and plumage have been labelled.

HONEY BUZZARD

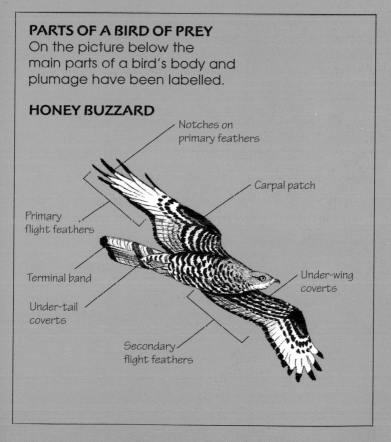

Notches on primary feathers

Carpal patch

Primary flight feathers

Terminal band

Under-tail coverts

Under-wing coverts

Secondary flight feathers

INTERNET LINKS

If you have access to the Internet, you can visit these websites to find out more about birds of prey. For links to these sites, go to the Usborne Quicklinks Website at **www.usborne-quicklinks.com** and enter the keywords "spotters birds of prey".

WEBSITE 1   Find information and audio and video clips of birds of prey on the website of the Royal Society for the Protection of Birds.

WEBSITE 2   Try fun activities online and find out about joining the RSPB Wildlife Explorers.

WEBSITE 3   Information, photos and audio clips of birds of prey on the Hawk Conservancy Trust site.

WEBSITE 4   Read about threats to birds of prey at the WWF Website.

WEBSITE 5   Learn about birds of prey around the world at the Peregrine Fund Website.

WEBSITE 6   Try to correctly place the birds of prey in a food chain game.

WEBSITE 7   Watch eagles on a live webcam.

WEBSITE 8   Browse webcam images of Peregrine falcons that nest each year on top of the Kodak Tower in the USA.

WEBSITE 9   Information, photos and audio clips of owls around the world.

SCORECARD

The birds of prey on this scorecard are arranged in alphabetical order. Fill in the date on which you spot a bird. Give yourself a score of 25 for any bird that is not on this list. Rare migrants occur in Britain and you may well see other raptors or owls if you visit other parts of Europe.

Species (Name of bird)	Score	Date spotted	Species (Name of bird)	Score	Date spotted
Buzzard	10		Kite, Red	15	
Buzzard, Honey	25		Merlin	20	
Buzzard, Rough-legged	25		Osprey	15	
Eagle, Golden	20		Owl, Barn	15	
Eagle, White-tailed	25		Owl, Little	10	
Goshawk	25		Owl, Long-eared	20	
Harrier, Hen	20		Owl, Short-eared	15	
Harrier, Marsh	15		Owl, Snowy	25	
Harrier, Montagu's	25		Owl, Tawny	5	
Hobby	20		Peregrine	20	
Kestrel	10		Sparrowhawk	10	

INDEX